This story is for my
T-Rrific little boy, Colin.
Daddy's love for you is
bigger than the biggest
T-Rex that ever walked on
this planet.
You are daddy's special
little boy and I love you
more and more each day.

There's a T-Rex in my bath tub and his name is Bubba Bub.

here's a T-Rex in my bath tub and all he says is glub, glub, glub.

3

There's a T-Rex in my bath tub who loves to splash water with its tail.

4

There's a T-Rex in my bath tub so there's no
room for an ostrich or a whale.

There's a T-Rex in my bath tub who hides under a face cloth.

There's a T-Rex in my bath tub who's
faster than a three toed sloth.

There's a T-Rex in my bath tub who sings with my daddy and me.

8

There's a T-Rex in my bath tub who eats
soap and apples from a tree.

There's a T-Rex in my bath tub whose giant
claws and scales are dripping wet.

There's a T-Rex in my bath tub and I'm glad
he's my only pre-historic pet.